MATCH OF THE ...

D0188338

Colour your
shirt in

Shirt
number

This book belongs to   Age

My favourite team is

My favourite player is

My highlight of 2019 was

ISLINGTON LIBRARIES

3 0120 02798295 8

WELCOME!

You can also catch up with MOTD on BBC iPlayer!

Don't forget to keep watching MOTD, readers!

WHAT A YEAR!

Wow, 2019 was a legendary year full of drama, excitement and epic footy. We'll look back at the highs and lows of the last 12 months, and look forward to 2020, which promises to be something special. Enjoy!

BBC One Don't miss *Match of the Day*, Saturdays and Sundays on BBC One and BBC Two!

96 PAGES OF FOOTY FUN!

WHAT'S INSIDE YOUR MOTD ANNUAL?

p7 A Star Is Born

p18 It's A Dog's Life Being A Baller

p22 Splash That Cash

I had a belter of a year!

DEAN SAYS:
"Mo Salah, Sadio Mane and Pierre-Emerick Aubameyang shared the Prem Golden Boot. They all tell me I'm the best ref in the world!"

DEAN SAYS:
"City walloped Watford in the FA Cup final! I reffed the 2008 final – people tell me it was the best refereeing display of all time!"

DEAN SAYS:
"Chelsea beat Arsenal 4-1 in the Europa League final – Eden Hazard scoring twice. Hazard tells me I'm the best ref he's ever seen!"

DEAN SAYS:
"Liverpool beat Tottenham 2-0 in the Champions League final. Jurgen Klopp tells me I'm the best ref in the history of football!"

DOUBLE ACT Man. City won their second consecutive top-flight title in 2018-19!

THE TOP 10 FOOTY MURALS!

p30 Mural, Mural, On The Wall...

THE WOMEN'S WORLD CUP

p38 Women's World Cup

MEGASTAR MANSION

p46 Welcome To The Megstars Mansion

THE A-Z OF TEKKERS!

p50 The A-Z Of Tekkers

PIERRE-EMERICK AUBAMEYANG

14

ARSENAL

Cut out & keep your fave posters!

★★★A STAR IS★★★
BORN!

FEATURING...
5 BRITS
3 BRAZILIANS
2 GERMANS
& 1 BIG CRAZY SWEDE!

Ladies and gentlemen, boys and girls, cats and dogs– it's time to reveal the best footballers born each year between **1981** and **2000**

TURN OVER FOR MORE!

1981
IN
FOOTBALL
ENGLISH CHAMPIONS:
Aston Villa
FA CUP WINNERS:
Tottenham
EUROPEAN CUP
WINNERS:
Liverpool

ZLATAN IBRAHIMOVIC
LA GALAXY

Friday 2 October 1981 was a pretty normal day in Malmo, Sweden's third-largest city. Dads were driving their Volvos, kids were eating meatballs and mums were singing along to Abba. But the next day, everything changed. The legend that is Zlatan Ibrahimovic was born – and life would never be the same again!

1982
IN
FOOTBALL
ENGLISH CHAMPIONS:
Liverpool
FA CUP WINNERS:
Tottenham
EUROPEAN CUP
WINNERS:
Aston Villa

KAKA
RETIRED

His birth certificate says Ricardo Izecson Dos Santos Leite – but we call him Kaka. Not only was the Brazilian attacking midfielder a joy to watch, he won every prize in the game in the mid-2000s. After being born in April 1982, he went on to play for Sao Paulo, AC Milan, Real Madrid and Orlando City in the MLS before retiring in 2017!

1983
IN
FOOTBALL
ENGLISH CHAMPIONS:
Liverpool
FA CUP WINNERS:
Man. United
EUROPEAN CUP
WINNERS:
Hamburg

DANI ALVES
SAO PAULO

1983 was a big year for world peace, long-distance running and Brazilian right-backs – that's because North Korea's Supreme Leader Kim Jong-Un, Olympic hero Mo Farah and Dani Alves were all born. However, only one of those 36-year-olds can claim to be the most decorated footballer of all time after winning more than 40 trophies in his career – and it's not that Kim fella!

ANDRES INIESTA
VISSEL KOBE

Two of the world's best centre-backs were born in 1984 – PSG's Thiago Silva and Juventus' Giorgio Chiellini. But neither are the best baller born that year – that's Spanish legend Andres Iniesta. He's playing in Japan now – but he was unreal when clocking up nearly 700 games for Barcelona from 2002 to 2018!

1984
IN
FOOTBALL
ENGLISH CHAMPIONS:
Liverpool
FA CUP WINNERS:
Everton
EUROPEAN CUP
WINNERS:
Liverpool

CRISTIANO RONALDO

JUVENTUS

The very first episode of EastEnders was broadcast in February of 1985 – but two weeks earlier an even more momentous thing happened. More than 1,500 miles away from Albert Square, on the Portuguese island of Madeira, Cristiano Ronaldo Dos Santos Aveiro was born – a man who's gone on to win almost 30 trophies, more than 100 individual awards and score nearly 700 goals. Unbelievable!

1985
— IN —
FOOTBALL
ENGLISH CHAMPIONS:
Everton
FA CUP WINNERS:
Man. United
EUROPEAN CUP WINNERS:
Juventus

TURN OVER FOR MORE!

DAVID SILVA
MAN. CITY

While Manchester was shivering in sub-zero temperatures at the start of 1986, in a sleepy fishing village on the sunshine holiday island of Gran Canaria, a future City legend arrived into the world. David Josue Jimenez Silva, who has now clocked up more than 400 games in England, is one of the best players the Premier League has ever seen!

1986
IN
FOOTBALL
ENGLISH CHAMPIONS:
Liverpool
FA CUP WINNERS:
Liverpool
EUROPEAN CUP WINNERS:
Steaua Bucharest

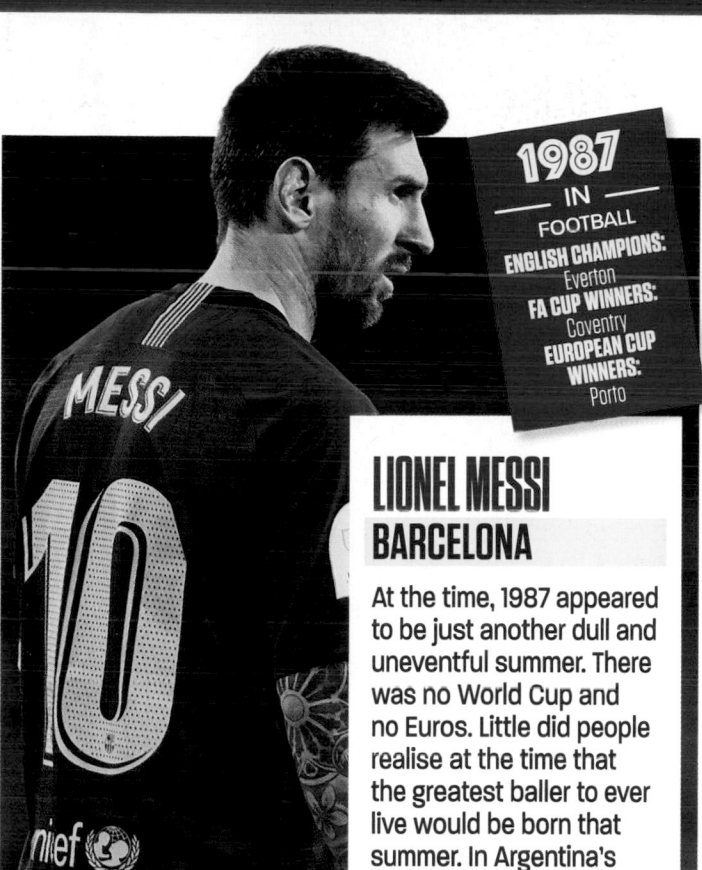

LIONEL MESSI
BARCELONA

1987
— IN —
FOOTBALL
ENGLISH CHAMPIONS:
Everton
FA CUP WINNERS:
Coventry
EUROPEAN CUP WINNERS:
Porto

At the time, 1987 appeared to be just another dull and uneventful summer. There was no World Cup and no Euros. Little did people realise at the time that the greatest baller to ever live would be born that summer. In Argentina's third-biggest city Rosario, on 24 June, Mr and Mrs Messi welcomed their little son Lionel into the world and football changed forever!

SERGIO AGUERO
MAN. CITY

1988
— IN —
FOOTBALL
ENGLISH CHAMPIONS:
Liverpool
FA CUP WINNERS:
Wimbledon
EUROPEAN CUP WINNERS:
PSV Eindhoven

In 1988, almost a year after Lionel Messi's birth, another future Argentina star was born, this time 300km away in the country's capital Buenos Aires. Fifteen years later Serge became the youngest player to play in the Argentine Primera Division and eight years after that he joined Man. City. He's since become an all-time Prem great with four titles and a Golden Boot!

GARETH BALE
REAL MADRID

1989
— IN —
FOOTBALL
ENGLISH CHAMPIONS:
Arsenal
FA CUP WINNERS:
Liverpool
EUROPEAN CUP WINNERS:
AC Milan

Two of the planet's most famous wizards were born in July 1989 – Harry Potter actor Daniel Radcliffe and Wales' very own footballing magician Gareth Bale. Both 29-year-olds have gone on to become global superstars, with Bale, for a while, being the world's most expensive ever player following his £89m move to Real Madrid in 2013!

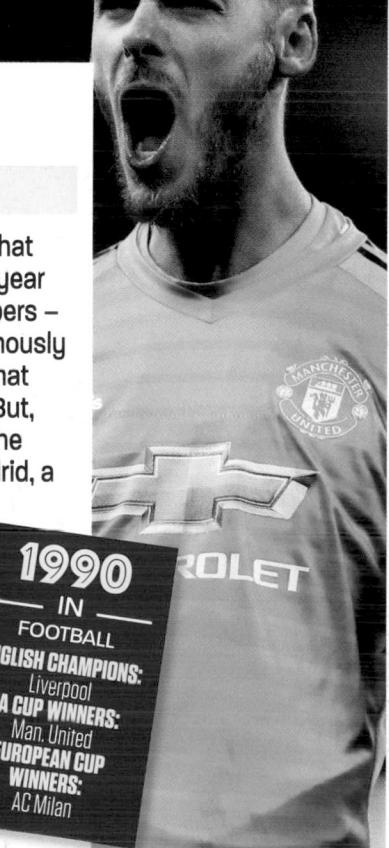

DAVID DE GEA
MAN. UNITED

Most people agree that 1990 wasn't a great year for Man. United keepers – No.1 Jim Leighton famously had a nightmare in that year's FA Cup final. But, six months later, in the Spanish capital Madrid, a baby boy called David was born who'd go on to become one of the club's all-time great goalkeepers – and also, quite possibly, the best in the world!

1990
— IN —
FOOTBALL
ENGLISH CHAMPIONS:
Liverpool
FA CUP WINNERS:
Man. United
EUROPEAN CUP WINNERS:
AC Milan

TURN OVER FOR MORE!

1991
— IN —
FOOTBALL
ENGLISH CHAMPIONS:
Arsenal
FA CUP WINNERS:
Tottenham
EUROPEAN CUP WINNERS:
Red Star Belgrade

EDEN HAZARD
REAL MADRID

Something wonderful happened across Europe in 1991 – five of the world's best players were born. Kevin De Bruyne, Antoine Griezmann, Virgil van Dijk and N'Golo Kante could all claim to be the best footballer born that year – but for sheer talent and for being sprinkled with a little more magic dust, Eden Hazard gets our vote as the year's standout baller!

1992
— IN —
FOOTBALL
ENGLISH CHAMPIONS:
Leeds
FA CUP WINNERS:
Liverpool
EUROPEAN CUP WINNERS:
Barcelona

NEYMAR
PSG

On 5 February 1992, C-Ron was celebrating his seventh birthday in his hometown of Funchal – but 7,000km away in Sao Paulo, Brazil, a couple were celebrating the birth of their son Neymar Da Silva Santos Junior. Twenty-five years later he would become the most expensive player ever when he joined PSG from Barcelona for almost £200m!

1993
— IN —
FOOTBALL
ENGLISH CHAMPIONS:
Man. United
FA CUP WINNERS:
Arsenal
UCL WINNERS:
Marseille

HARRY KANE
TOTTENHAM

It's May 1993 and Spurs fans are celebrating the fact their star frontman Teddy Sheringham has just won the Prem Golden Boot for the 1992-93 season. But there would be something even bigger for them to celebrate two months later – the birth of their superstar striker and England captain Harry Kane, the best player to be born that year!

RAHEEM STERLING
MAN. CITY

1994 wasn't one of the greatest seasons in Man. City's history – they finished 16th in the Premier League, were dumped out of the FA Cup by third-tier Cardiff and bitter rivals Man. United won the title! But what fans didn't know at the time is that four of their future heroes were all born this year – Aymeric Laporte, John Stones, Bernardo Silva and, the best of the lot, Raheem Sterling!

1994
— IN —
FOOTBALL
ENGLISH CHAMPIONS:
Man. United
FA CUP WINNERS:
Man. United
UCL WINNERS:
AC Milan

JOSHUA KIMMICH

BAYERN MUNICH

This is the year Woody and Buzz made their first appearance on the big screen in the original *Toy Story* – it's also the year little baby Joshua arrived. Twenty-four years on and the versatile full-back/midfielder, who's already won four Bundesliga titles, two German Cups and 42 caps for Germany, has become a vital player for club and country!

1995
— IN —
FOOTBALL
ENGLISH CHAMPIONS:
Blackburn
FA CUP WINNERS:
Everton
UCL WINNERS:
Ajax

TURN OVER FOR MORE!

LEROY SANE

MAN. CITY

It's safe to say 1996 was a memorable year for German football. The national team, much to English heartbreak, won Euro 96 at Wembley, Bayern Munich won what is now the Europa League and in Essen, an old coal mining city in the west of the country, this flying forward was born. Sane has developed into one of the game's most dynamic and dangerous attackers!

1996 IN FOOTBALL

ENGLISH CHAMPIONS:
Man. United

FA CUP WINNERS:
Man. United

UCL WINNERS:
Juventus

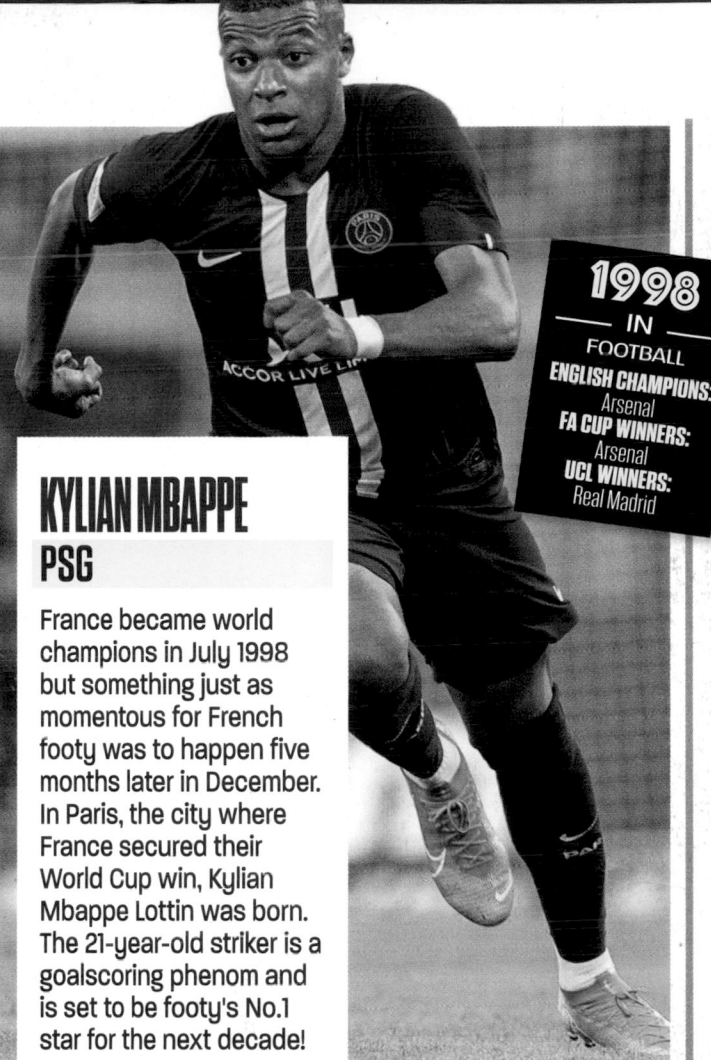

1997
IN
FOOTBALL
ENGLISH CHAMPIONS:
Man. United
FA CUP WINNERS:
Chelsea
UCL WINNERS:
Borussia Dortmund

1998
IN
FOOTBALL
ENGLISH CHAMPIONS:
Arsenal
FA CUP WINNERS:
Arsenal
UCL WINNERS:
Real Madrid

MARCUS RASHFORD
MAN. UNITED

Five months after Man. United had won their fourth Premier League title in five years, just down the road from Old Trafford, a future hero was born. Marcus Rashford, who's now 22, has already played nearly 200 games – and in every one of those games he's skinned every defender he's come up against. Rashford is pure danger on the football pitch!

KYLIAN MBAPPE
PSG

France became world champions in July 1998 but something just as momentous for French footy was to happen five months later in December. In Paris, the city where France secured their World Cup win, Kylian Mbappe Lottin was born. The 21-year-old striker is a goalscoring phenom and is set to be footy's No.1 star for the next decade!

1999
IN
FOOTBALL
ENGLISH CHAMPIONS:
Man. United
FA CUP WINNERS:
Man. United
UCL WINNERS:
Man United

2000
IN
FOOTBALL
ENGLISH CHAMPIONS:
Man. United
FA CUP WINNERS:
Chelsea
UCL WINNERS:
Real Madrid

MATTHIJS DE LIGT
JUVENTUS

It's incredible to think this 20-year-old centre-back was born in 1999 – he has the maturity and physicality of a player born ten years earlier. De Ligt, schooled at Ajax and now being fine-tuned at Juve, will be the world's dominant centre-back for the next ten years – meaning his £76m transfer fee could be an absolute steal!

JADON SANCHO
BORUSSIA DORTMUND

2000 was a bad summer for English footy as Kevin Keegan's England team crashed out of Euro 2000 in the group stage – torn apart by a skilful Portugal team and a clinical Romania. Little did anyone know that three months earlier, in a south-London hospital, a baby was born who'd become more skilful and more clinical than those two opponents. That baby was Jadon Malik Sancho!

A YEAR IN FOOTBALL!

How much can you remember about 2019? Let's find out...

HOW DID YOU DO?
TURN TO p92 FOR THE ANSWERS!

1

Who was PFA Player of the Year last season?

A Raheem Sterling ☐
B Virgil van Dijk ☐
C Mohamed Salah ☐

2

What was the score in the FA Cup final?

A Man. City 4-0 Watford ☐
B Man. City 5-0 Watford ☐
C Man. City 6-0 Watford ☐

3

Who scored the first goal in last season's Champions League final?

A Sadio Mane ☐
B Mohamed Salah ☐
C Roberto Firmino ☐

4

Who finished third in the Premier League last season?

A Arsenal ☐
B Chelsea ☐
C Tottenham ☐

5

Which city hosted the Europa League final?

A Madrid ☐
B Baku ☐
C Bucharest ☐

6

Which Man. United player made the 2018-19 PFA Team of the Year?

A David De Gea ☐
B Paul Pogba ☐
C Marcus Rashford ☐

7

Which club did Real Madrid sign Luka Jovic from earlier this year?

A PSV Eindhoven ☐
B Eintracht Frankfurt ☐
C Lille ☐

8

Who was the top-scoring English player in the Prem last term?

A Raheem Sterling ☐
B Jamie Vardy ☐
C Harry Kane ☐

9

Who won the 2019 UEFA Nations League in June?

A England ☐
B Portugal ☐
C Holland ☐

ANTOINE GRIEZMANN

BARCELONA

Cut out & keep your fave posters!

MATCH of the DAY magazine

MATCH OF THE DAY IN ASSCIATION
WITH SNAPPY SNAPS PRESENTS...

FOOTBALL
THE MOVIE!

You probably lie awake at night wondering what it would be like if Hollywood was full of dog actors who made a movie about footy. Wonder no more – we've found the perfect dogs to play the biggest stars!

STARRING
CARLOS THE CHIHUAHUA
AS BRAZIL ICON
NEYMAR

AND
HECTOR THE CHIHUAHUA
AS MAN. UNITED
& ENGLAND JOKER
JESSE LINGARD

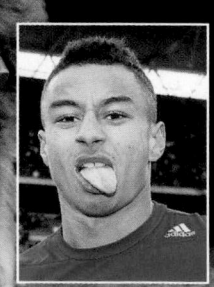

WITH
LARRY THE LABRADOODLE
AS ARSENAL
CENTRE-BACK
DAVID LUIZ

ALSO STARRING
RORY THE IRISH TERRIER
AS BARCELONA
LEGEND
LIONEL MESSI

AND
**SAMMY THE STAFFORDSHIRE
BULL TERRIER**
AS CAGLIARI TOUGH GUY
RADJA NAINGGOLAN

WITH
**PEDRO THE PORTUGUESE
WATER DOG**
AS LIVERPOOL HERO
MOHAMED SALAH

FEATURING
PABLO THE PULI
AS REAL MADRID
& BRAZIL ACE
MARCELO

WITH
**GORDON THE
GOLDEN RETRIEVER**
AS LIVERPOOL MANAGER
JURGEN KLOPP

AND
**BARRINGTON THIRLWELL-
SMITH THE POODLE**
AS **PIERRE-EMERICK
AUBAMEYANG**

ALSO STARRING
HENRY THE HAVANESE PUPPY
AS ENGLAND &
EVERTON KEEPER
JORDAN PICKFORD

AND INTRODUCING
MARIO THE MALTESE PUPPY
AS MAN. CITY
GOAL KING
SERGIO AGUERO

COMING TO CINEMAS
NEAR YOU... NEVER!

THE CHAMPIONS QUIZ!

Just tick the team you think has won the most titles in the major European leagues below!

HOW DID YOU DO? TURN TO p92 FOR THE ANSWERS!

1 ENGLAND

A Liverpool
B Man. City
C Man. United

2 GERMANY

A Borussia Dortmund
B Bayern Munich
C Schalke

3 SPAIN

A Real Madrid
B Sevilla
C Barcelona

4 ITALY

SERIE A
TI

A Juventus
B AC Milan
C Inter Milan

5 SCOTLAND

SCOTTISH PREMIERSHIP

A Rangers
B Celtic
C Aberdeen

6 BELGIUM

Jupiler
LEAGUE

A Genk
B Club Brugge
C Anderlecht

7 TURKEY

SüperLig

A Fenerbahce
B Galatasaray
C Besiktas

8 HOLLAND

A Feyenoord
B PSV
C Ajax

9 PORTUGAL

A Porto
B Bcnfioo
C Sporting Lisbon

Cut out & keep your fave posters!

2

LUCY
BRONZE
ENGLAND

$ILLY MON

THE STORY OF THE WORLD TRANSFER RECORD!

Back in 1975, Giuseppe Savoldi became football's first £1m player when he moved from Bologna to Napoli. Since then the world transfer record has been smashed 21 times – let's take a look at each of those deals!

£198m

TURN OVER FOR MORE!

GIUSEPPE SAVOLDI
Bologna to Napoli
£1.2m — 1975

The 28-year-old Italy striker was one of Serie A's most feared frontmen when Napoli signed him. He won the Italian Cup in his first season at the Stadio San Paolo and scored 55 goals in 118 games before re-joining Bologna four years later!

PAOLO ROSSI
Juventus to Vicenza
1976

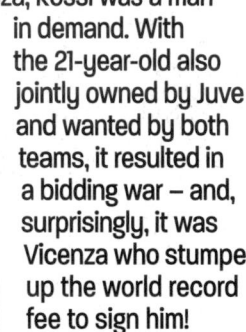

Having won two Golden Boots in two years with Vicenza, Rossi was a man in demand. With the 21-year-old also jointly owned by Juve and wanted by both teams, it resulted in a bidding war – and, surprisingly, it was Vicenza who stumped up the world record fee to sign him!

£1.75m

RUUD GULLIT
PSV to AC Milan
1987

The 24-year-old attacker had just been named Dutch Footballer of the Year when AC Milan lured him to Italy. He won the Ballon d'Or, three Serie A titles and two European Cups in his six years before joining Sampdoria in 1993!

£6m

DIEGO MARADONA
£3m

Boca Juniors to Barcelona 1982

The iconic No.10 was a highly rated 21-year-old when he moved to the Nou Camp from his homeland Argentina in 1982. Despite scoring 38 goals in 58 games and winning the Copa Del Rey, injury and controversy plagued Maradona's short spell at Barcelona – he fell out with club chiefs and was sold to Serie A club Napoli in 1984!

Barcelona to Napoli 1984

Maradona's big-money move to Naples saw him break the transfer record for the second time in two years – and it saw him produce the most magical football of his illustrious career. He led Napoli to their most successful ever period – winning two Serie A titles, the Italian Cup and the UEFA Cup in a memorable seven-year spell over in Italy!

£5m

ROBERTO BAGGIO
Fiorentina to Juventus
1990

During a five-year spell at Fiorentina, 23-year-old Baggio had become one of football's most-wanted stars – resulting in this record-breaking move to Juventus. The Divine Ponytail, as he was known, won Serie A, the Italian Cup, the UEFA Cup and the Ballon d'Or in his five seasons with Juventus before he was sold to AC Milan in 1995!

£8m

JEAN-PIERRE PAPIN
Marseille to AC Milan
1992

The 29-year-old striker had been Ligue 1's biggest star and top scorer for the past five seasons, he'd fired Marseille to four titles in a row and was the reigning Ballon d'Or holder when Milan broke the bank to sign him. However, the Frenchman struggled in Serie A and after two disappointing seasons he left to join Bayern Munich!

£10m

GIANLUCA VIALLI
Sampdoria to Juventus
1992

After eight goal-packed seasons at Sampdoria, where he won three Italian cups, the league, the European Cup Winners' Cup and the Serie A Golden Boot, Vialli moved to Juventus. He spent four years in Turin, winning the title and the Champions League, before joining Chelsea in 1996!

£12m

GIANLUIGI LENTINI
Torino to AC Milan
1992

The transfer record was smashed for the third time in a year when Milan splashed out big bucks for Torino's 23-year-old winger Gianluigi Lentini. The skilful Italian won the league in his first season, but a year after signing was involved in a serious car crash. He never fully recovered and loft for Atalanta in 1996!

£13m

RONALDO
PSV Eindhoven to Barcelona 1996

The original Ronaldo, aged just 20, had rattled in 54 goals in 57 games over two seasons for PSV Eindhoven in the Dutch league when he sealed his move to Barca. The Brazil striker continued his red-hot form in Spain, being named FIFA World Player of the Year after scoring 47 goals in his one and only season at the Nou Camp before surprisingly quitting the club to join Italian giants Inter Milan!

£13.2m

ALAN SHEARER
Blackburn to Newcastle 1996

After netting 130 goals in 171 games for Blackburn over four seasons and top scoring at Euro 96, 25-year-old Shearer made a momentous move to his hometown team Newcastle, who'd finished second In the Premier League the previous season. The English striker wrote his name into the history books over the next decade at St James' Park – becoming the Premier League's all-time record goalscorer. Legendary!

£15m

RONALDO
Barcelona to Inter Milan 1997

Just 12 months after moving to Barcelona, the Brazilian joined Inter for a then world record fee, making him only the second player, after Diego Maradona, to break the transfer record twice. He hit 59 goals in 99 games, was named Serie A Footballer of the Year and won the Ballon d'Or as he established himself as the world's best striker. But after injuries hampered his final seasons with Inter, he left for Real Madrid in 2002 for £28m!

£19.5m

TURN OVER FOR MORE!

DENILSON
Sao Paulo to Real Betis   1998

It was another Brazilian who claimed the transfer record from Ronaldo – this time Sao Paulo's 21-year-old winger Denilson. But the tricky wideman, famed for his elaborate stepovers, struggled to live up to his massive price tag and after seven unspectacular seasons at Betis, where he scored 13 goals in 186 games, he was sold to Bordeaux for an undisclosed fee!

£21.5m

KAKA
AC Milan to Real Madrid   2009

£56m

It took eight years for the Zidane transfer fee to be beaten – and it was Real Madrid once again who flexed their financial muscle. In a six-year spell at AC Milan, Brazilian star Kaka had proved to be one of the game's elite attacking midfielders, winning every team and individual honour. However, after four injury-ravaged, disappointing seasons in Spain he returned to Milan in 2013!

CHRISTIAN VIERI
Lazio to Inter Milan   1999

Two years after breaking the transfer record to sign Ronaldo, Inter Milan were at it again – this time bagging 26-year-old Italy striker Christian Vieri. Inter were Vieri's ninth club in nine seasons, which included spells at Juventus and Atletico Madrid. He scored 123 goals in six years with Inter – before making a shock move to city rivals AC Milan in 2005!

£32.5m

LUIS FIGO
Barcelona to Real Madrid   2000

Crespo only held the record for a matter of days before 29-year-old Portugal winger Luis Figo became the world's most expensive player in one of the most controversial transfers ever. After five glorious years with Barcelona, he moved to bitter rivals Real Madrid, where he won two titles, the UCL and the Ballon d'Or in five seasons!

£37m

£35.5m

HERNAN CRESPO
Parma to Lazio   2000

A year after selling their own star striker Vieri, Lazio splashed out a record amount on his replacement – Parma's Argentina hitman Hernan Crespo. He won the Serie A Golden Boot in his first season, but was sold to Inter two years later with Lazio in finanical trouble!

ZINEDINE ZIDANE
Juventus to Real Madrid   2001

A year after breaking the record to sign Figo, Real smashed it again by signing another global superstar – France No.10 Zinedine Zidane. The 29-year-old had become one of the greatest players of his generation during five years in Italy – but over the next five seasons he confirmed himself as one of the best of all time, winning La Liga, the Champions League and the Ballon d'Or. He played more than 200 games for Real, before retiring in 2006!

£46.5m

CRISTIANO RONALDO

£80m

Man. United to Real Madrid 2013

Less than a month after smashing the eight-year-old transfer record, Real did it again when they completed the spectacular signing of Man. United's Cristiano Ronaldo, the reigning World Player of the Year. Over the next decade, the 24-year-old would become a football legend – scoring 450 goals in 438 games on his way to winning four UCL titles and four Ballons d'Ors!

GARETH BALE

£86m

Tottenham to Real Madrid 2013

For the fifth time in a row it was Real Madrid who proved to be the ultimate big spenders – as they made the 24-year-old Welsh wizard the world's most expensive player. Bale, who'd just been named PFA Player of the Year after scoring 26 goals in 44 games for Tottenham, penned a six-year deal at the Bernabeu. Despite an injury-hit six seasons at Real, he's still won four UCL titles and La Liga!

PAUL POGBA

Juventus to Man. United 2016

For the first time in 20 years, since Alan Shearer's move to Newcastle, an English club smashed the world transfer record. This time it was when Man. United stumped up almost £90m for a player who left them for nothing four years earlier. Pogba, who'd matured into one of the game's top CMs in his time in Italy, won the Europa League and EFL Cup in his first season back at Old Trafford and made the PFA Team of the Year last season!

£89m

NEYMAR

£198m

Barcelona to PSG 2017

In August 2017, Brazil superstar Neymar became the most expensive player in footy history when he moved to French giants PSG. The 25-year-old had been part of a formidable attack at Barcelona, alongside Lionel Messi and Luis Suarez, winning trophies galore. But the lure of huge wages and a dream of winning the Ballon d'Or saw him swap life in Spain for the French capital. He's since won two league titles, the French Cup and been named Ligue 1 Player of the Year!

TROPHY HUNTERS!

How long is it since each Premier League club won a major trophy? Let's take a look...

Club	Time	Last major trophy
Liverpool	LESS THAN ONE YEAR	Champions League, 2019
Chelsea	LESS THAN ONE YEAR	Europa League, 2019
Man. City	LESS THAN ONE YEAR	FA Cup, 2019
Man. United	TWO YEARS	Europa League, 2017
Arsenal	TWO YEARS	FA Cup, 2017
Leicester	THREE YEARS	Premier League, 2016
Tottenham	11 YEARS	League Cup, 2008
Aston Villa	23 YEARS	League Cup, 1996
Everton	24 YEARS	FA Cup, 1995
Norwich	34 YEARS	League Cup, 1985
West Ham	39 YEARS	FA Cup, 1980
Wolves	39 YEARS	League Cup, 1980
Southampton	43 YEARS	FA Cup, 1976
Newcastle	50 YEARS	Fairs Cup*, 1969
Burnley	59 YEARS	Division One**, 1960
Sheffield United	94 YEARS	FA Cup, 1925
Bournemouth	n/a	never won a major trophy
Brighton	n/a	never won a major trophy
Crystal Palace	n/a	never won a major trophy
Watford	n/a	never won a major trophy

PAZ SAYS
*The Fairs Cup is the old name for the Europa League – and **Division One is what the Prem used to called!

MATCH of the DAY magazine

Cut out & keep your fave posters!

REAL MADRID
LUKA JOVIC

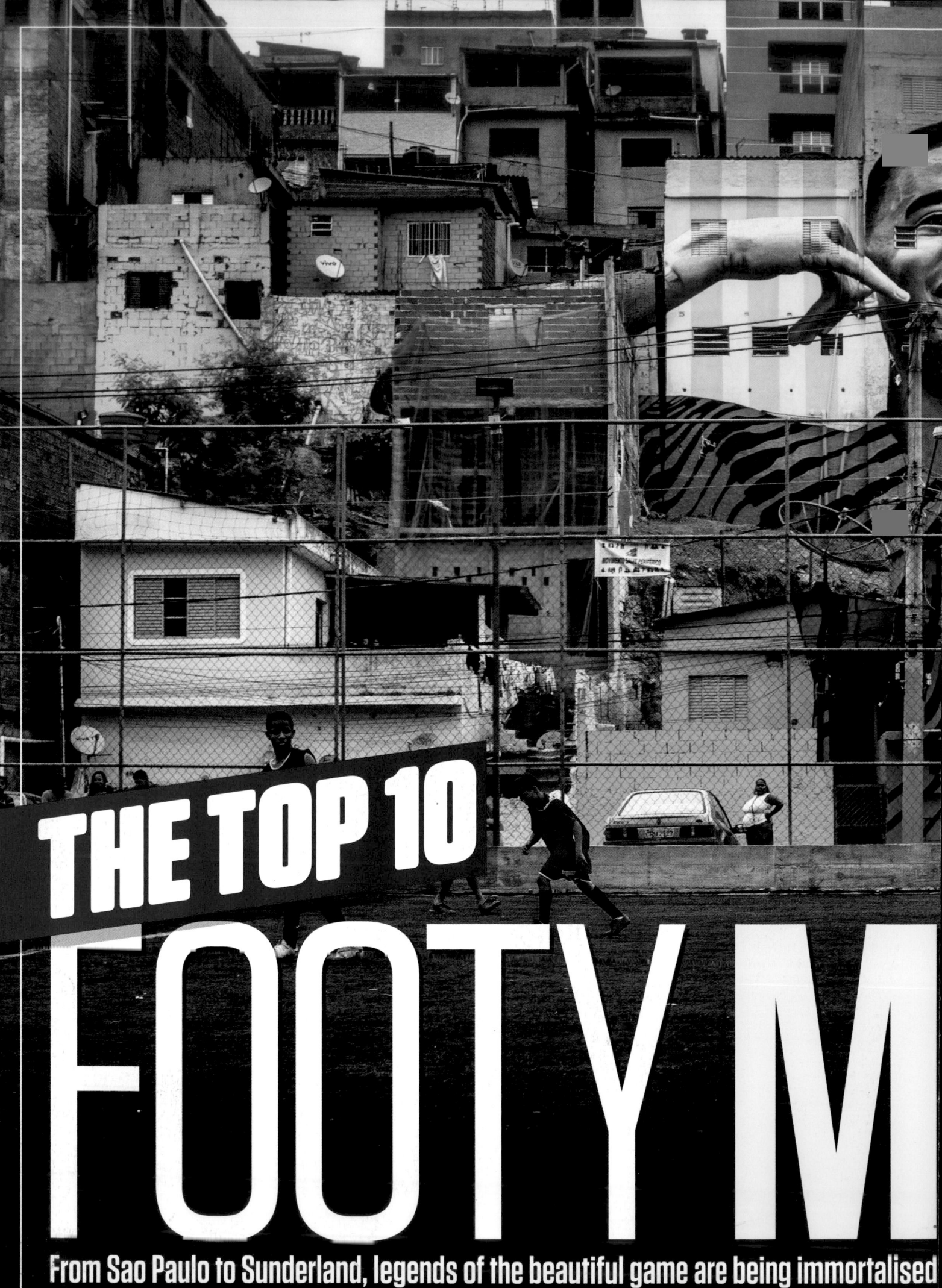

THE TOP 10
FOOTY M

From Sao Paulo to Sunderland, legends of the beautiful game are being immortalised

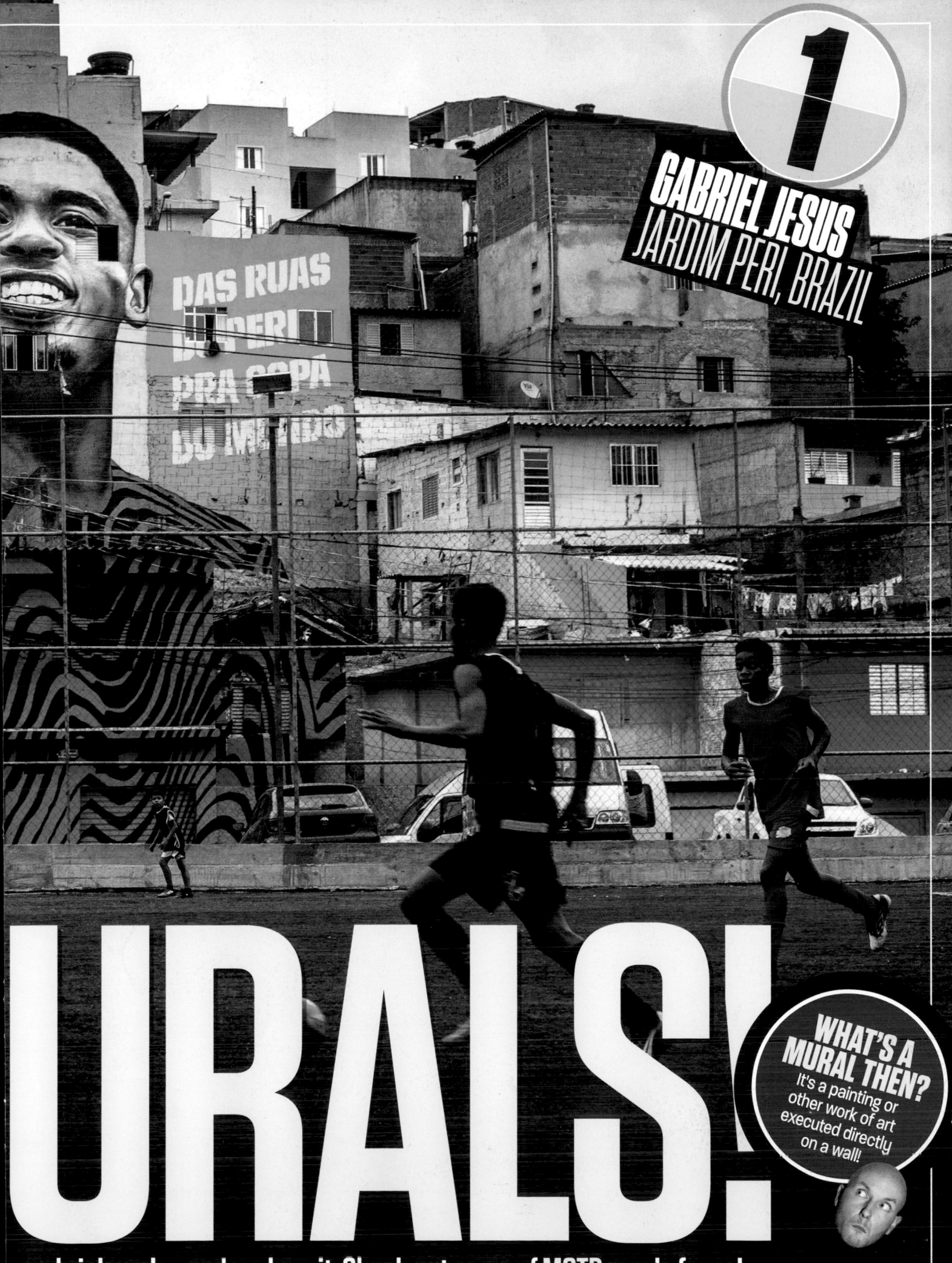

1 GABRIEL JESUS
JARDIM PERI, BRAZIL

WHAT'S A MURAL THEN?
It's a painting or other work of art executed directly on a wall!

URALS!

on brickwork – and we love it. Check out some of MOTD mag's faves!

TURN OVER FOR MORE!

2 MO SALAH
CAIRO, EGYPT

4 MATCH OF THE CENTURY
ENGLAND 3-6 HUNGARY, 1953
BUDAPEST, HUNGARY

3 LIONEL MESSI
ROSARIO, ARGENTINA

5 RAICH CARTER
HENDON, SUNDERLAND

6

JURGEN KLOPP
JORDAN STREET,
LIVERPOOL

WE ARE LIVERPOOL.
THIS MEANS MORE.

7 BRUNO
CHURCH STREET,
BRIGHTON

Capitán

8

CRISTIANO RONALDO
KAZAN, RUSSIA

9

IAN MUIR & RAY MATHIAS
PRENTON PARK, BIRKENHEAD

10

DIEGO MARADONA
NAPLES, ITALY

mars

GUESS WHO?

HOW DID YOU DO? TURN TO p92 FOR THE ANSWERS!

Just name these Prem ballers from their profiles below!

PLAYER 1

NAME: ....

Born:		Romford, England
Date of birth:		27 February 1992 (age 27)

YEARS	TEAM	GAMES/GOALS
2008–2010	Charlton	42/7
2010–2013	Liverpool	47/2
2011	Blackpool (loan)	10/6
2013–2016	Swansea	79/10
2016–	Newcastle	103/7

PLAYER 2

NAME: ....

Born:		Glasgow, Scotland
Date of birth:		11 March 1994 (age 25)

YEARS	TEAM	GAMES/GOALS
2012–2013	Queen's Park	34/2
2013–2014	Dundee United	36/3
2014–2017	Hull	99/3
2017–	Liverpool	58/1

PLAYER 3

NAME: ....

Born:		Agen, France
Date of birth:		27 May 1994 (age 25)

YEARS	TEAM	GAMES/GOALS
2011–2012	Basconia	33/2
2012	Bilbao Athletic	8/0
2012–2018	Athletic Bilbao	161/7
2018–	Man. City	44/3

PLAYER 4

NAME: ....

Born:		Bietigheim-Bissingen, Germany
Date of birth:		4 March 1992 (age 27)

YEARS	TEAM	GAMES/GOALS
2009–2011	Stuttgart II	57/0
2011–2018	Bayer Leverkusen	233/0
2018–	Arsenal	32/0

PLAYER 5

NAME: ....

Born:		Liverpool, England
Date of birth:		25 February 1993 (age 26)

YEARS	TEAM	GAMES/GOALS
2012–2014	Liverpool	1/0
2013–2014	Sheff. United (loan)	39/5
2014–2015	Huddersfield	45/3
2015–	Wolves	160/1

PLAYER 6

NAME: ....

Born:		Meaux, France
Date of birth:		20 July 1993 (age 25)

YEARS	TEAM	GAMES/GOALS
2010–2011	Lille B	36/1
2011–2013	Lille	49/2
2013–2016	PSG	29/0
2015–2016	Roma (loan)	33/3
2016–2018	Barcelona	29/0
2018–	Everton	35/4

Kante

Cut out & keep your fave posters!

CHELSEA

FRANCE

football *noun*
foot·ball | \ 'fut-,bȯl \
Definition of football
1 : a game played between two teams usually on a rectangular field having goalposts or goals at each end and whose object is to get the ball over a goal line, into a goal, or between goalposts by running, passing, or kicking

This is Lionel **Messi** – the best footballer of all time

This is a ball – you need to kick it

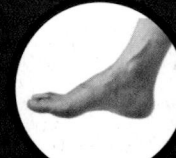

This is a foot – you kick the ball with this

You need to kick the ball into this – it's a goal

Do NOT kick this – it is a cow. It won't like being kicked

If you kick the cow, **Farmer Jones** will chase you and put you in a pie

These are **hands**. You CANNOT use these unless you're a goalkeeper

This is a goalkeeper

IMPORTANT Do not mix them up!

This is a zookeeper

This is a stadium – this is where football matches are played

This is a park – you can have a kickabout with friends here

This is a volcano – this is NOT a place to play football

Football is more than 150 years old – in the olden days players were black and white

RTER PACK!

What's that? Some people in your class don't like football? Sit them down, show them this page and educate them on the beautiful game!

NO. THIS IS WRONG. THIS IS AMERICAN FOOTBALL

YES. THIS IS RIGHT. THIS IS REAL FOOTBALL

This is a referee – you WILL see these on a football pitch

This is a proboscis monkey – you will NOT see these on a football pitch

This is a foul

This is a fowl

Who's got my egg?

This is an orangutan – he can't play football

This is an aardvark – he can't play football

This is a pie – it's a traditional half-time snack

This is a toilet brush – it's not a traditional half-time snack

This is Phil Jones – he can't play football

THE WOM[I]

Goals, tekkers, tea, spies, skills, fights, fun, pens, passion

EN'S WORLD CUP

TURN OVER FOR MORE!

and some other VAR-y big moments – this one had the lot!

UN-FOUR-TUNATE START (FOR KOREA!)

➥ Hosts France beat South Korea 4-0 on the opening night – the tournament is up and running!

BATTLE OF BRITAIN!

➥ England narrowly beat Scotland 2-1 with a pen from Nikita Parris, an Ellen White goal – and the assistance of VAR!

UNLUCKY 13!

➥ Tourney faves USA do THIS 13 times to poor Thailand – 13-0, ouch!

RAIN STOPS PLAY!

➥ It gets so wet at Roazhon Park that the ref takes both teams off. Sweden nick a group-stage win over Chile when it eventually dries!

HARD LINES, SCOTLAND!

➥ Scotland (needing a win to make the last 16) are 3-0 up v Argentina, but draw 3-3! Lee Alexander saves a late pen but VAR orders a retake!

PERFECT THREE LIONESSES!

➥ England top their group with maximum points – the first time they've won all three group games in their history!

AUSTRALIA PAY THE PENALTY!

➡ The first pen shootout of the World Cup sees Norway dramatically dump Australia out of the tourney in the last-16 stage!

PAZ SAYS
Australia were one of the pre-tournament faves – this was the first major shock of the comp!

KEEP CALM AND BEAT CAMEROON!

➡ Cameroon almost quit their last-16 game v England in a huff over VAR calls that go against them. England keep their cool and win 3-0!

HAPPY HOSTS!

➡ France see off a strong Brazil team 2-1 in extra-time to keep their World Cup dream alive!

TURN OVER FOR MORE!

IS IT COMING HOME?

England stroll past Norway 3-0 to book a semi-final place against the mighty USA. Eek!

KETCH SAYS
Team MOTD mag watched this game together – we went nuts when Jill Scott scored the opener!

RUTHLESS RAPINOE!

A Megan Rapinoe free-kick worms its way into the France net early on prompting another iconic cele. The USA win 2-1 to book their semi spot!

HANDY FOR HOLLAND!

A harsh ball-to-hand VAR call in the dying minutes gives Holland an opportunity to book a semi-final place for the first time in their history – they take it at the expense of Japan!

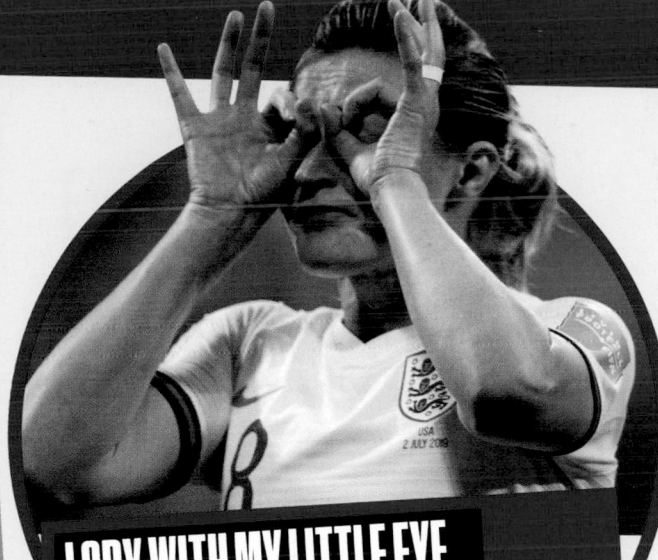

I SPY WITH MY LITTLE EYE...

➘ USA staff members are spotted in England's hotel ahead of their semi v The Lionesses. The officials claim they were scouting the venue in case they made the final! Hmmm...

DOWN TO A TEA!

➘ Alex Morgan celebrates what turns out to be a semi-final winner by pretending to drink some English tea! England's heartache isn't helped by an 82nd-minute pen miss by captain Steph Houghton!

HOW MANY?!

➘ A peak audience of 11.7 million Brits tune in to watch England's brave 2-1 semi-final defeat – the most-watched TV programme of 2019. A huge breakthrough for women's football!

EXTRA SPECIAL!

➘ Man. United midfielder Jackie Groenen's sweet extra-time strike settles their cagey semi-final against Sweden. Holland make their first ever women's final. #scenes!

NO BRONZE FOR LUCY!

➘ England start slowly in their bronze medal game v Sweden and lose 2-1. Lucy Bronze finishes an incredible tourney in style, though!

A FOURTH STAR!

➘ It takes an hour, but Rapinoe scores the penalty that sets USA on the way to their fourth World Cup win, her sixth tournament goal and the Golden Ball for the comp's best player – it finishes USA 2-0 Holland!

MOTD SCRAPBOOK QUIZ

How many famous faces can you guess from our five-star photoshoots?

1

2

3

4

5

6

7

HOW DID YOU DO? TURN TO p92 FOR THE ANSWERS!

STARS ♥ MOTD

8

9

10

11

12

13

14

15

16

17

18

19

20

MEGAST★R MANSION

Rubber duck

The FA Cup

Maradona toy

Tennis ball

A mouse

Golden boot

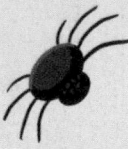
A spider

Mesut Özil

Spurs bottle

Can you find these 9 hidden items in the picture?

MAN. CITY
PREMIER LEAGUE CHAMPIONS

2018-19 LEAGUE

JUVENTUS
SERIE A CHAMPIONS

PSG
LIGUE 1 CHAMPIONS

BAYERN MUNICH
BUNDESLIGA CHAMPIONS

BARCELONA
LA LIGA CHAMPIONS

WINNERS!

CELTIC
SCOTTISH PREM CHAMPIONS

Ladbrokes

Ladbrokes
PREMIERSHIP

2018/19 WINNERS

CELTIC FOOTBALL CLUB

THE A-Z OF TEKKERS!

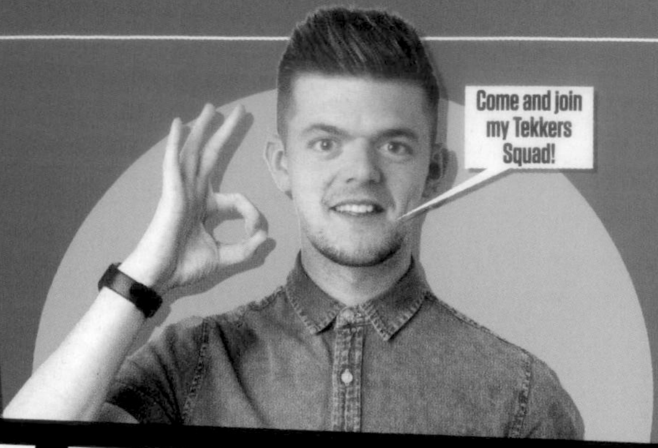
Come and join my Tekkers Squad!

From whippage to rabonas, level up your skills knowledge with our go-to guide!

A IS FOR... Around the world

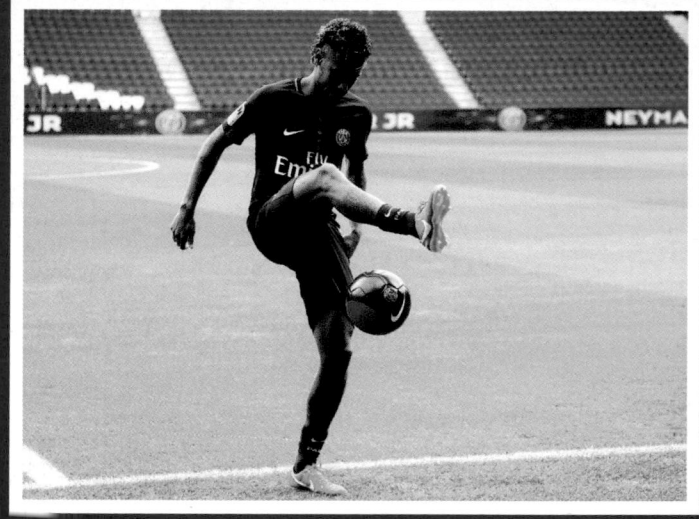

While keeping the ball up, lightly spin it using the outside of your foot, before sharply lifting your leg up, over and around the ball, only to catch it on your touch again. It's the skill that upgrades your basic keepy-uppies!

NEYMA
JR
Fly Emirates

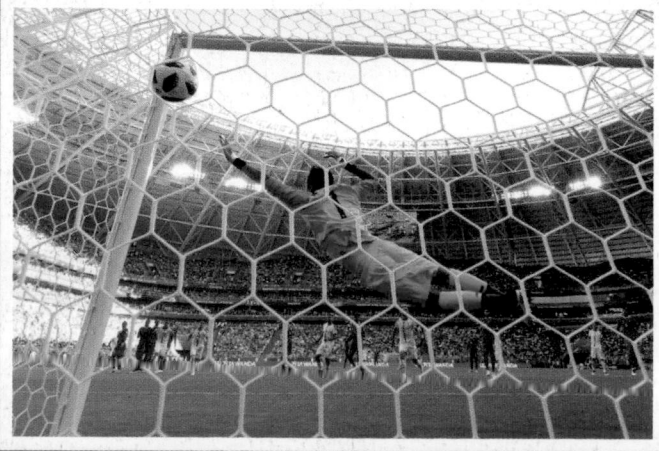

B IS FOR... Bins

No, not where you chuck your used banana skins, but either the top or bottom corners of the goal. Trust us, when you slap the top bins with a sledgehammer shot, you'll know it. The crowd will be on a madness!

C IS FOR... Cruyff Turn

Legendary Dutch baller Johan Cruyff, who the skill is named after, first busted this out against Sweden in the 1974 World Cup. It's been bamboozling defenders ever since and is so iconic, it has its own Wikipedia page!

E IS FOR... Elastico

Created by Barcelona legend Ronaldinho – but executed by very few! On the dribble, you flick the ball one way and chop it back the other, all in one sharp movement to send the defender flying for a sandwich!

D IS FOR... Diag

A crossfield ball that zips diagonally across the pitch, usually from the centre-back or centre-mid to a winger or flying full-back. David Lulz absolutely loves bringing this out!

F IS FOR... Five-star baller

A player with tonnes and tonnes of awesome attributes. Someone who can head, tackle and strike zinger burgers in their sleep. Only the very best players ever get given this title. And it's earned, never given!

TURN OVER FOR MORE!

G IS FOR... Goal

The best feeling in footy! Nothing beats the vibe you get when the ball hits the back of the net. Trust, we even get buzzed off consolation goals when we're losing. Ha!

H IS FOR... Hat-trick

Scoring one goal is ledge, bagging two is a real buzz, but netting THREE in one game – a hat-trick – is ultimate levels! Better yet, a perfect hatty, consisting of left foot, right foot and headed finishes will place you in an elite goals squad!

I IS FOR... Intelligence

No player ever got anywhere by just running around the pitch like a headless chicken. Learn the game, study your position and then put your findings into action. Know who to play the pass to, when to shoot and how to use your body!

K IS FOR... Knuckleball

A type of free-kick using low spin and mind-blowing zigzag trajectory that makes it impossible for keepers to predict. Cristiano Ronaldo is the king of this tek – check his free-kick for Man. United against Portsmouth in 2008!

O IS FOR...

L IS FOR... Last-minute winner

When the clock is ticking, the game is getting away from you and a point is not what your team wants, popping up with a goal in the final few seconds is only topped by one thing – the scenes after you score!

Overhead kick

When the ball is flying through the air into the box, you could jump up and head it – OR you could leap up with your back to goal, perform a scissor-like action with your legs and strike towards goal with your strong foot Gareth Bale-style!

J IS FOR... Jockey

It hasn't always got to be a slide, you know? Sometimes, when defending, it's best to be patient by jockeying the opponent– shuffling side on – and jab-tackling the ball away when the opportunity presents itself!

M IS FOR... Mindset

If your attitude stinks, your play will hum, too! Be positive, willing to learn and always encourage your team-mates. The best ballers play most of the game in their head!

N IS FOR... Nutmeg

Also known as a panna, the nutmeg is when you slyly pop the ball through an opponent's legs. Stay clever and keep those legs together, readers!

TURN OVER FOR MORE!

P IS FOR... Panenka

A piece of tekkers used when taking a penalty, in which the taker delicately dinks it down the middle instead of wrapping it into the corner. It's named after former Czech player Antonin Panenka, who did this for the first time at Euro '76!

Q IS FOR... Quaresma

Portuguese baller Ricardo Quaresma doesn't score many, but when he does, he busts out his very own skill shot – the trivela, which is where you strike the ball using the outside of your foot to add lots of whippage. Whoosh!

R IS FOR... Rabona

Argentinian Ricardo Infante of Estudiantes first landed the rabona in 1948. It's where a player connects with the ball by wrapping their kicking leg around the back of their standing leg like a cross!

T IS FOR... Teknicians

This is YOU! Yes, YOU, reading these words RIGHT NOW! Whether you're a regular reader of MOTD mag or this is your first time, you are all part of Stobbsy's Tekkers Squad. Keep working hard and reap the rewards!

S IS FOR... Swaz

Created by F2 ballers Billy and Jez, swaz is when you cut across the ball using the outside of your foot to generate a left-to-right twist while it's in flight!

U Under control
IS FOR...

When the ball is pinging about all over the pitch, you need a player with the composure to kill the ball dead and get it under control to settle the team down. Head, chest, knee or in-step – it doesn't matter what you use, control is key!

V VAR
IS FOR...

No, it's not specifically about tekkers itself, but a new element of gameplay that all elite-level ballers need to be aware of if they want to reach the very top and smash their goals!

W Whippage
IS FOR...

Another word for curling the ball – usually used for crossing or with direct free-kicks. Wrap your foot right around the ball so it curls well away from the opposition!

X X-ray vision
IS FOR...

You know them midfielders that play passes you didn't even see were on? Yeah, them ones right there – this one is a shout-out to them. They can see through players and paint pictures of plays on the pitch before they've happened. Think Kevin De Bruyne!

Y Young ballers
IS FOR...

Wonderkids are where it's at and where all the new-gen skill moves are being born. Some of the best young players in the world like Jadon Sancho and Kylian Mbappe are showing everyone tek they've never seen before. Give youth a chance!

Z Zing
IS FOR...

That feeling when you connect with the ball so sweetly, it almost makes a whistle sound through the air. One of those where it doesn't matter if it goes flying over the bar, it just felt ledge!

Listen to live Premier League games on BBC Radio 5 live

WHAT'S THE BEST RICE?

Rice, rice, baby – do, do-do, doo, do-do-do, do!

A royal Rice rumble today, folks. One is a pro baller for West Ham and England – the other a takeaway classic. But which one is best?

DECLAN RICE or EGG FRIED RICE?

DECLAN RICE	SCORE		SCORE	EGG FRIED RICE
Born in Kingston upon Thames, south-west London, in January 1999, Declan is 20 years old	2	AGE	10	The earliest record of fried rice is from China during the Sui dynasty in 600AD
We've never licked Dec – and he wouldn't want us to. But he looks like he'd taste of sweat and corned beef. Yuck!	1	TASTE	8	Lovely. Perfect with a Chinese chicken curry and some prawn crackers
You'd not get much change from £50m in today's transfer market	9	COST	1	£3.50 down at our local takeaway Wok This Way
Only six players made more tackles than Declan in the Premier League last season	8	TACKLING	0	It's rice – it's not exactly gonna two-foot you, is it?
Not a natural goalscorer	0	GOALSCORING	0	Not a natural goalscorer
Very popular in east London (West Ham territory). Not very popular in the Republic Of Ireland	5	POPULARITY	8	Eaten globally and particularly popular in Asia – but our nan think it tastes like muck
Declan is 1.85m tall, which is just over 6ft. He's pretty big	8	SIZE	1	A grain of rice is a bit bigger than a fat ant but much smaller than a slug

Dec scored well in most categories apart from goalscoring and taste but he did enough to claim a clear win over his Chinese rival

33 FINAL SCORES **28**

The rice's football ability really let it down here today – if it can work on that, it could well topple Declan as the Rice King

7J

RONALDO

Cut out & keep your fave posters!

J U V E N T U S

PLAY TIM

E!

Absolute scenes down at the playground – we've never seen anything like it!

WHERE'S WARNOCK?
The Cardiff boss is hiding! But where is he?

KYLIAN

PARIS   SAINT-GERMAIN

MBAPPE

Cut out & keep your fave posters!

MATCH of the DAY
magazine

THE WEIRD & WONDERFUL FOOTY QUIZ!

ZOIKS!

WARNING!
Not your normal brainteasers!

Sometimes the beautiful game gets a bit weird, and sometimes it's just plain wonderful! This bonkers quiz is a bit of both – *LET'S GET CRACKING!*

TURN OVER FOR MORE!

THE WEIRD ROUND!

HOW DID YOU DO? TURN TO p92 FOR THE ANSWERS!

1 What did Fred Davies use to retrieve balls kicked out of Shrewsbury's old ground?

A A boat ☑ B A dog ☑ C A bike ☑ D A lasso ☑

2 What were all three goalscorers in the 2008 League Cup final wearing?

 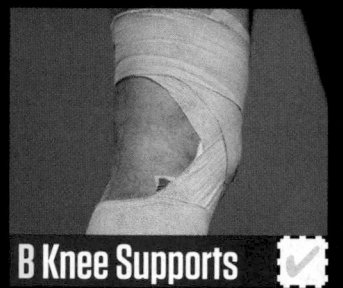  

A Facemasks ☑ B Knee Supports ☑ C Goggles ☑ D Headbands ☑

3 Which of these Scottish football clubs is mentioned in The Bible?

A Queen Of The South ☑ B Celtic ☑ C St Johnstone ☑ D Alloa ☑

4

Former England Under-21 player Curtis Woodhouse quit football aged 26 to take up which sport?

A Horseracing ☑ B Gymnastics ☑
C Boxing ☑ D Golf ☑

5 Why was Nottingham Forest v Tottenham abandoned after 14 minutes in 1996?

A Snow ☑ B Red cards ☑
C Ref Injury ☑ D Pitch invasion ☑

6  In other languages it's known as kolo, cano, mata nuki and petite pont – what is it in English?

A Handball

B Nutmeg

C Backheel

D Offside

7  How many players can a team have sent off before a match is abandoned?

A Three

B Four

C Five

D Six

8 Which of these Americans once took part in the League Cup draw?

 A Beyonce

 B Muhammad Ali

 C Donald Trump

 D Homer Simpson

9 Which sport legend made his pro football debut for an Australian team in 2018?

 A Usain Bolt

 B Roger Federer

 C Tiger Woods

 D LeBron James

10 Which ex-Prem player called their autobiography *How To Be A Footballer*?

 A Frank Lampard

 B Robbie Savage

 C Rob Green

 D Peter Crouch

TURN OVER FOR MORE!

HOW DID YOU DO? TURN TO p92 FOR THE ANSWERS!

11 Which British team has won the European Cup more times than its own top league?

A Aston Villa

B Liverpool

C Rangers

D Nott'm Forest

12 Who is the oldest goalscorer in Premier League history?

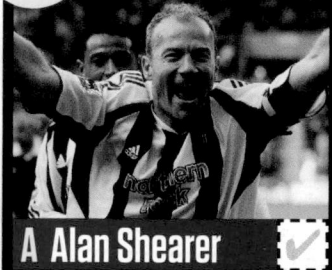
A Alan Shearer

B Z. Ibrahimovic

C T. Sheringham

D Jermain Defoe

13 Which baller has played in the north London, Merseyside and Manchester derbies?

A Robin van Persie

B Wayne Rooney

C Thierry Henry

D Nicolas Anelka

14 How old was Cristiano Ronaldo when he became captain of Portugal?

A 18
B 22
C 25
D 30

15 Which club has had a player on the pitch in every World Cup final since 1982?

A Juventus

B Man. United

C Bayern Munich

D Real Madrid

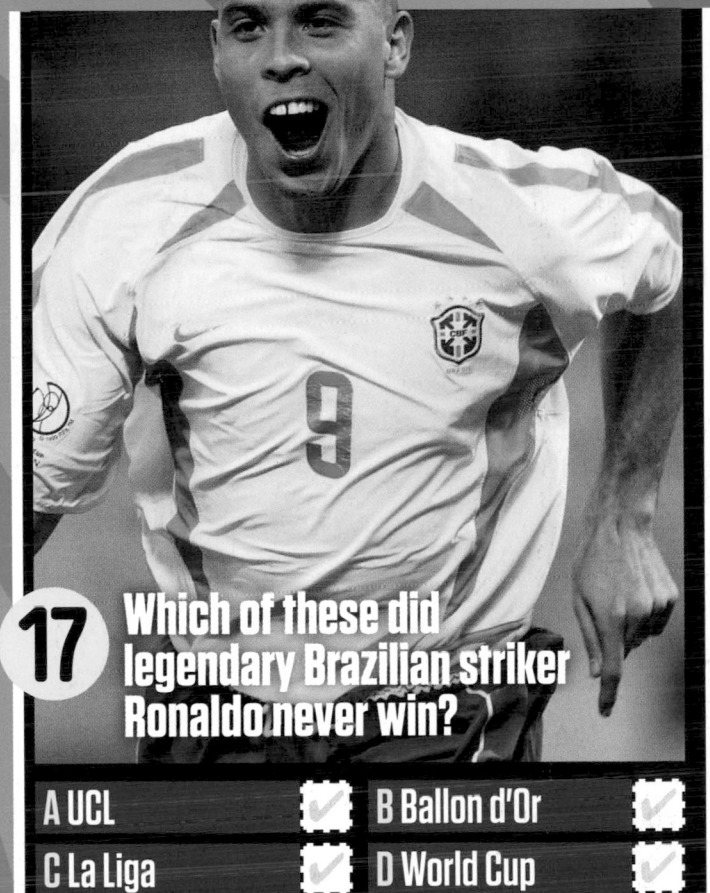

16 Lionel Messi holds the record for most football game cover appearances – how many is it?

A Eight

B 11

C 19

D 36

17 Which of these did legendary Brazilian striker Ronaldo never win?

A UCL

B Ballon d'Or

C La Liga

D World Cup

18 Which Scandinavian national team have Brazil never beaten?

A Sweden

B Denmark

C Norway

D Finland

19 Along with Cristiano Ronaldo, who has scored in UCL finals for two different clubs?

A Samuel Eto'o

B Filippo Inzaghi

C Mario Mandzukic

D Divock Origi

20 Which Scottish team doesn't contain any of the letters used in the word

FOOTBALL

17

KEVIN DE BRUYNE
MAN.CITY

Cut out & keep your fave posters!

MATCH of the **DAY** magazine

JOAO FELIX
ATLETICO MADRID

Cut out & keep your fave posters!

SACKED IN THE

✂ CUT OUT THE HEADS AND PLACE 👉

UNAI EMERY
Arsenal

DEAN SMITH
Aston Villa

EDDIE HOWE
Bournemouth

GRAHAM POTTER
Brighton

SEAN DYCHE
Burnley

FRANK LAMPARD
Chelsea

ROY HODGSON
Crystal Palace

MARCO SILVA
Everton

BRENDAN RODGERS
Leicester

JURGEN KLOPP
Liverpool

PEP GUARDIOLA
Man. City

OLE GUNNAR SOLSKJAER
Man. United

STEVE BRUCE
Newcastle

DANIEL FARKE
Norwich

CHRIS WILDER
Sheffield United

RALPH HASENHUTTL
Southampton

MAURICIO POCHETTINO
Tottenham

JAVI GRACIA
Watford

MANUEL PELLEGRINI
West Ham

NUNO ESPIRITO SANTO
Wolves

All managers correct at time of going to press!

MORNING

the boot – now you have to decide what job he does next!

WHAT YOU NEED TO DO!

With the help of an adult, cut out the heads of the Premier League bosses and then place them onto the bodies on this page!

WHO ARE YOU?

Ever wondered which footy star you are? Well, just take our little quiz and you'll soon find out!

Q1 YOU'VE FOUND AN EGG – WHAT DO YOU DO WITH IT?

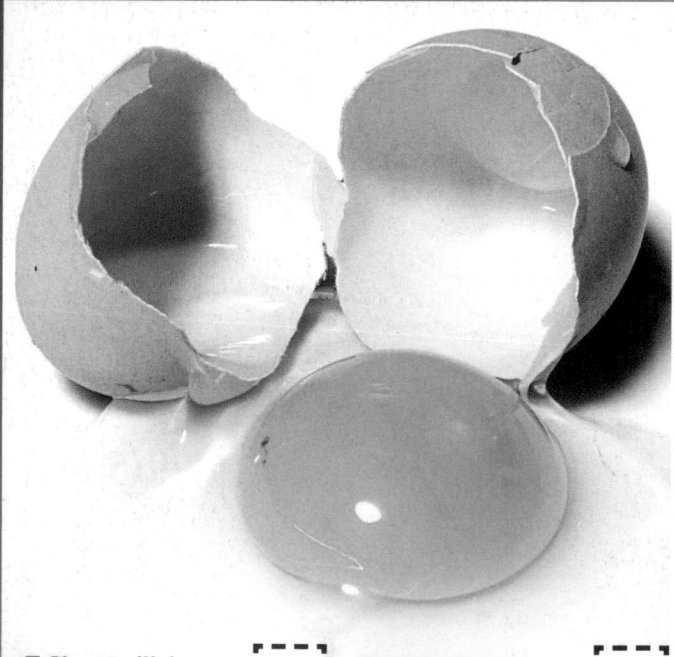

A Film yourself balancing it on your head!

B Add it to your extensive collection of eggs!

C Bake yourself a lovely cake. Mmmm, cake!

D Give it a little sniff – then eat it!

Q2 YOU'VE POPPED IN TO TOWN – WHICH SHOP DO YOU HEAD TO FIRST?

A Louis Vuitton – for some exclusive threads!

B The Garden centre – to look at the plants!

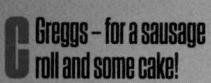

C Greggs – for a sausage roll and some cake!

D Forget the shops – you've found a bin to rummage in!

Q3 YOU'RE OUT ON THE TRAINING PITCH – WHAT ARE YOU DOING?

A Chilling out, doing some keepy-uppies!

B Starting your second 5km run of the day!

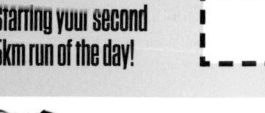

C Just finishing off a slice of chocolate cake!

D Chomping on a discarded shinpad!

Q4 IT'S TIME FOR SOME LUNCH – WHAT'S ON THE MENU?

A Chicken and veg prepared by your own chef!

B Plain cheese sandwich and a cup of tea!

C Lemon cheesecake and a strawberry trifle!

D An old slipper you've found under the table!

Q5 YOU'RE RELAXING AT HOME – WHAT ARE YOU UP TO?

A In your home cinema playing *FIFA 20*!

B Binge-watching *Antiques Roadshow*!

C In your dressing gown eating a chocolate eclair!

D Munching on a bunch of flowers you discovered!

Q6 THERE'S A KNOCK AT THE DOOR – WHO IS IT?

A A load of mates have come to play five-a-side!

B The insurance man you invited round for a chat!

C The baker delivering your box of fresh cakes!

D You're too busy eating the carpet to hear it!

SO, HOW DID YOU ANSWER?

MOSTLY As

You are Neymar
You're flashy, confident and enjoying the fame and fortune that comes with being a world-class footballer!

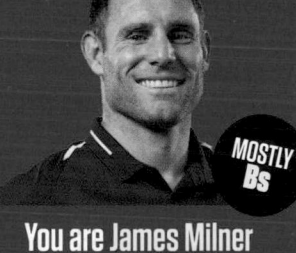

MOSTLY Bs

You are James Milner
Some call you boring – but you're just, er, sensible. Nothing fancy, nothing flamboyant – just, er, sensible!

MOSTLY Cs

You are Steve Bruce
We all like cake – but we don't like it as much as you like it! Maybe spend some of that cake time focusing on footy!

MOSTLY Ds

You are a goat
Hang on, you're not a player or a boss – you're a goat! What are you doing here? You can't even read!

QUIZ A GROWN-UP!

HOW DID THEY DO?
TURN TO p92 FOR THE ANSWERS!

Go grab mum, dad or someone else who's basically an oldie – it's time for you to put them to the test!

1

Which Premier League club did this man manage in the 1995-96 season?

A Norwich

B Blackburn

C Arsenal

2 Name this football legend from the profile below!

DATE OF BIRTH:		1 February 1969 (age 50)
PLACE OF BIRTH:		Avellaneda, Santa Fe, Argentina
YEARS	TEAM	GAMES/GOALS
1988–1989	Newell's Old Boys	16/4
1989–1990	River Plate	19/3
1990–1991	Boca Juniors	30/13
1991–2000	Fiorentina	269/168
2000–2003	Roma	63/30
2003	Inter Milan (loan)	12/2
2003–2005	Al-Arabi	21/25

NAME:

3

Which USA '94 World Cup star is this?

NAME:

4

Four Italian managers have won the Premier League – name them all!

1

2

3

4

6 Name the two England internationals pictured here in 1991!

NAME: / NAME:

5

Which two teams are pictured here from a match in the early days of the Premier League?

TEAM A:

TEAM B:

FINAL SCORE	0-4	Ha-ha! They need to buy you a treat!
/11	5-8	Not bad – but not good enough, grown-up!
	9-11	Sorry, quizmaster – the adult gets control of the TV for the whole day!

MATCH of the DAY

Cut out & keep your fave posters!

MATCH of the **DAY**
magazine

MADE IN MANCHESTER

10

MARCUS RASHFORD

WSL 2019
DREAM TEAM!

MOTD mag brings you an epic 11 made up of the best ballers from the Women's Super League campaign over the past year!

SOPHIE BAGGALEY Keeper
Bristol City

LISA EVANS Right-back
Arsenal

STEPH HOUGHTON Centre-back
Man. City

LEAH WILLIAMSON Centre-back
Arsenal

DEMI STOKES Left-back
Man. City

BAGGALEY

EVANS HOUGHTON WILLIAMSON STOKES

WALSH JI VAN DE DONK

MEAD MIEDEMA CUTHBERT

KEIRA WALSH Midfielder
Man. City

SO-YUN JI Midfielder
Chelsea

DANIELLE VAN DE DONK Midfielder
Arsenal

BETH MEAD Forward
Arsenal

ERIN CUTHBERT Forward
Chelsea

VIVIANNE MIEDEMA Striker
Arsenal

Watch WSL games live on the BBC Sport website and BBC iPlayer BBC iPlayer

THE 5-A-SIDE WORLD CUP!

We've picked dream teams from each continent – which do YOU think is the best?

EUROPE

DE GEA
SPAIN

VAN DIJK
HOLLAND

DE BRUYNE
BELGIUM

MBAPPE
FRANCE

RONALDO
PORTUGAL

AFRICA

ONANA
CAMEROON

KOULIBALY
SENEGAL

GUEYE
SENEGAL

SALAH
EGYPT

AUBAMEYANG
GABON

ASIA

BEIRANVAND
IRAN

HASEBE
JAPAN

KI
SOUTH KOREA

LEI
CHINA

SON
SOUTH KOREA

SOUTH AMERICA

EDERSON
BRAZIL

SILVA
BRAZIL

FERNANDINHO
BRAZIL

MESSI
ARGENTINA

NEYMAR
BRAZIL

NORTH & CENTRAL AMERICA

NAVAS
COSTA RICA

ALVAREZ
MEXICO

HERRERA
MEXICO

JIMENEZ
MEXICO

PULISIC
USA

THE TEAMS RANKED!

Rank the five-a-side teams above in order – starting with the best continent and ending with the worst!

1 ....
2 ....
3 ....
4 ....
5 ....

HE'S OUR CENTRE-HALF,
HE'S OUR No.4,
WATCH HIM DEFEND,
AND WE WATCH
HIM SCORE,
HE'LL PASS THE BALL,
CALM AS YOU LIKE,
HE'S...

VIRGIL VAN DIJK

4

Cut out & keep your fave posters!

global | /ˈɡləʊb(ə)l/ | *adjective*
1. relating to the whole world; worldwide.

THE GLOBAL ELITE!

The time for talking is over. We can reveal, once and for all, who truly are the greatest footballers in the world – AND WHO IS THE BEST OF THE BEST...

elite | /eɪˈliːt,ɪˈliːt/ | *noun*
1. a select group that is superior in terms of ability or qualities to the rest of a group or society.

TURN OVER FOR MORE!

KEEPERS

■ AGILE, COMMANDING AND BRAVE
■ EXPERT DECISION MAKER WITH PERFECT PASSING
■ INTELLIGENT, AWARE AND WITH LIGHTNING REFLEXES

1 JAN OBLAK
Atletico Madrid | Slovenia | 26 years old

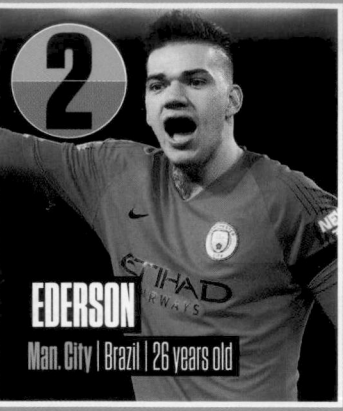

2 EDERSON
Man. City | Brazil | 26 years old

3 ALISSON BECKER
Liverpool | Brazil | 26 years old

4 DAVID DE GEA
Man. United | Spain | 28 years old

5 MARC-ANDRE TER STEGEN
Barcelona | Germany | 27 years old

FULL-BACKS

■ ENERGETIC, QUICK AND SUPER-FIT
■ EXCELLENT DRIBBLING, PASSING AND CROSSING SKILLS
■ TACTICALLY AWARE WITH POSITIONAL INTELLIGENCE

1 JOSHUA KIMMICH
Bayern Munich | Germany | 24 years old

2 JORDI ALBA
Barcelona | Spain | 30 years old

3 DAVID ALABA
Bayern Munich | Austria | 27 years old

4 TRENT ALEXANDER-ARNOLD
Liverpool | England | 20 years old

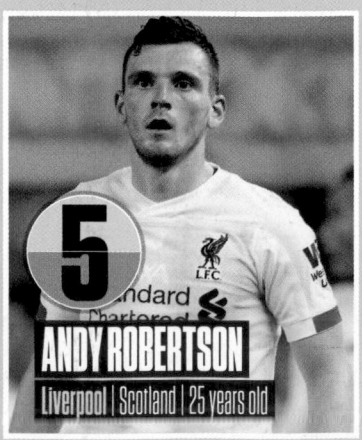

5 ANDY ROBERTSON
Liverpool | Scotland | 25 years old

CENTRE-BACKS

- COOL, CALM AND COMPOSED
- BIG, POWERFUL AND STRONG
- TACTICALLY AND TECHNICALLY EXCELLENT

1 VIRGIL VAN DIJK
Liverpool | Holland | 28 years old

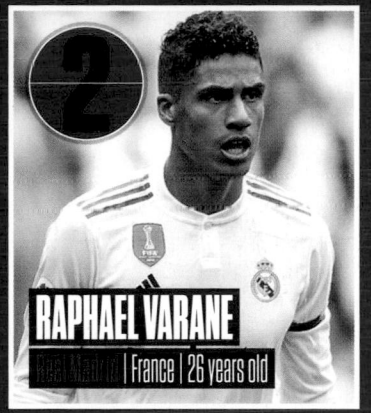

2 RAPHAEL VARANE
Real Madrid | France | 26 years old

3 SERGIO RAMOS
Real Madrid | Spain | 33 years old

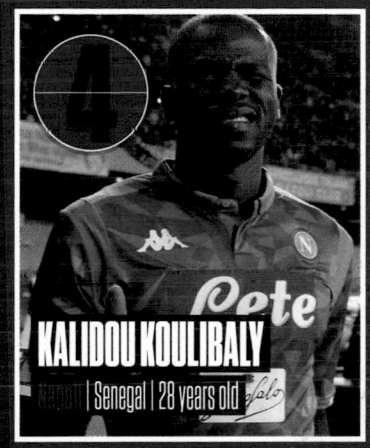

4 KALIDOU KOULIBALY
Napoli | Senegal | 28 years old

5 MATTHIJS DE LIGT
Juventus | Holland | 20 years old

MIDFIELDERS

- GREAT BALANCE, VISION AND CLOSE CONTROL
- CONFIDENT, INVENTIVE AND TECHNICALLY GIFTED
- A CREATIVE AND INTELLIGENT PASSER

1 KEVIN DE BRUYNE
Man. City | Belgium | 28 years old

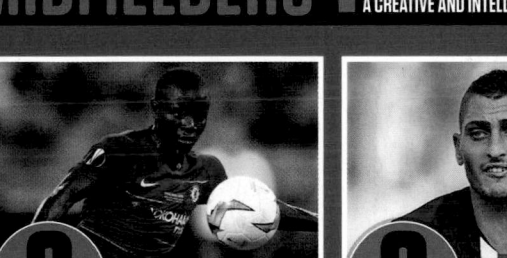

2 N'GOLO KANTE
Chelsea | France | 28 years old

3 MARCO VERRATTI
PSG | Italy | 26 years old

4 THIAGO ALCANTARA
Bayern Munich | Spain | 28 years old

5 PAUL POGBA
Man. United | France | 26 years old

TURN OVER FOR MORE!

FORWARDS

- QUICK-FEET WITH A LOCKER FULL OF TRICKS
- AMAZING CONTROL, TECHNIQUE AND VISION
- CREATES GOALS, SCORES GOALS – A GAME-CHANGER

1 LIONEL MESSI
Barcelona | Argentina | 32 years old

2 NEYMAR
PSG | Brazil | 27 years old

3 EDEN HAZARD
Real Madrid | Belgium | 28 years old

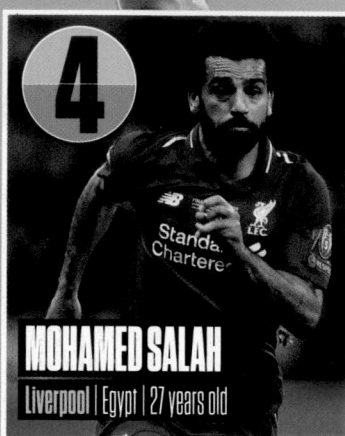

4 MOHAMED SALAH
Liverpool | Egypt | 27 years old

5 ANTOINE GRIEZMANN
Barcelona | France | 28 years old

STRIKERS

- THUNDEROUS SHOT AND SICK TECHNIQUE
- CLINICAL AND ICE-COOL IN FRONT OF GOAL
- OUTSTANDING MOVEMENT AND PENALTY BOX AWARENESS

1 CRISTIANO RONALDO
Juventus | Portugal | 34 years old

2 KYLIAN MBAPPE
PSG | France | 20 years old

3 HARRY KANE
Tottenham | England | 25 years old

4 SERGIO AGUERO
Man. City | Argentina | 31 years old

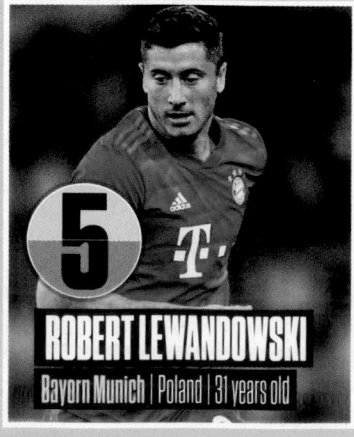

5 ROBERT LEWANDOWSKI
Bayern Munich | Poland | 31 years old

MANAGERS

- TACTICAL INTELLIGENCE AND FOOTBALL KNOWLEDGE
- A GREAT MAN-MANAGER WITH AN ABILITY TO MOTIVATE
- PHENOMENAL LEADERSHIP SKILLS

1 PEP GUARDIOLA
Man. City

2 JURGEN KLOPP
Liverpool

3 MAURICIO POCHETTINO
Tottenham

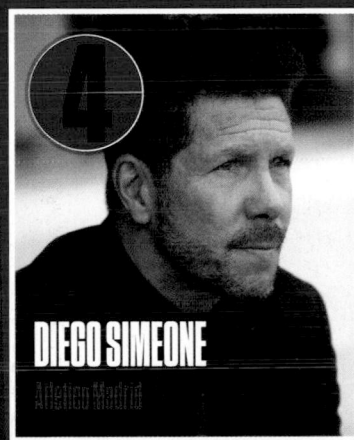

4 DIEGO SIMEONE
Atletico Madrid

5 MASSIMILIANO ALLEGRI
No club

WOMEN PLAYERS

- BAGS OF NATURAL ABILITY
- TOP-LEVEL DISPLAYS ON THE BIGGEST STAGE
- CONSISTENT PERFORMANCE

1 ADA HEGERBERG
LYON | NORWAY | 24 YEARS OLD

2 SAM KERR
Perth Glory / Chicago Red Stars
| Australia | 26 years old

3 PERNILLE HARDER
Wolfsburg | Denmark | 26 years old

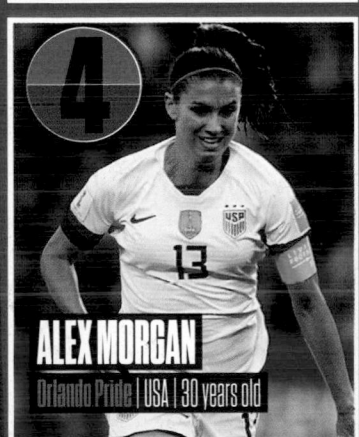

4 ALEX MORGAN
Orlando Pride | USA | 30 years old

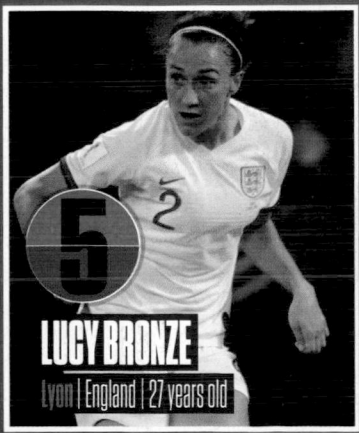

5 LUCY BRONZE
Lyon | England | 27 years old

ALEX MORGAN

USA

Cut out & keep your fave posters!

MATCH of the DAY magazine

Cut out & keep your fave posters!

JADON SANCHO

BORUSSIA DORTMUND

READER OFFER

NEVER MISS AN ISSUE OF

MATCH of the **DAY** magazine

OFFER DEADLINE DATE 31 JULY 2020

◆ PAY ONLY £4 for your first 4 issues!

◆ CONTINUE TO SAVE 21%* after your trial!

◆ DELIVERY DIRECT TO YOUR DOOR every week!

◆ NEVER MISS AN ISSUE of your favourite footy mag!

VISIT buysubscriptions.com/MDPSANN19

CALL 03330 162 126† QUOTE MDPSANN19

Closing date: 31 July 2020. Offer is only available for delivery to UK addresses and for UK Direct Debit customers. You will pay £?? 99 every three months but you may cancel at any time.
*The basic annual rate of Match of the Day is £11? per annum. Prices are discounted from the basic annual rate and include P&P. Subject to availability. †UK calls will cost the same as other standard fixed line numbers (starting 01 or 02) and are included in inclusive or free minutes allowances. Outside of free call packages, calls from mobile phones will cost between 3p and 55p per minute. Lines are open 8am-8pm weekdays and 9am-1pm Saturday.

SON HEUNG-M7N

TOTTENHAM

Cut out & keep your fave posters!

20 THINGS
YOU NEED TO KNOW ABOUT
EURO 2020

UEFA EURO 2016

1 PORTUGAL ARE THE HOLDERS!

Cristiano Ronaldo's crew are the current champions of Europe after their epic 2016 performance. Who can forget that mad 109th-minute extra-time winner from Eder!

2 IT'S BEING PLAYED IN 12 COUNTRIES!

It's the 60th birthday of the European Championships, so UEFA wanted to do something super special to celebrate. For the first time ever, 2020's tournament will be hosted in a dozen countries – England, Germany, Italy, Azerbaijan, Russia, Romania, Holland, Ireland, Spain, Hungary, Scotland and Denmark!

3 IT'S THE 16TH EUROS TOURNEY!

There have been a total of ten different winners in the past, but no country has triumphed more than both Germany and Spain – they've both lifted the trophy three times in their history!

4 EURO 2020 WILL LAST ONE MONTH!

If you're anything like us, you'll hate it when the season finishes, but who cares when there's an international tourney on? The Euros last one whole month from 12 June to 12 July. Pow!

5 THE FINAL IS AT WEMBLEY!

Not only will London's Wembley Stadium host three group games, one knockout round and both semi-finals, but it'll also welcome the two top teams for the grand final. Proper ledge!

6 VAR WILL BE IN PLAY!

It's got its fair share of haters, but no one can deny the entertainment VAR brought to 2018's World Cup in France, so we're buzzing that it'll be used for the first ever time at a European Championship!

7 MEET THE MASCOT – SKILLZY!

Mascots always bring LOL banter. Over the years, there's been The Rabbit in 1992, Slavek and Slavko in 2012, but 2020 is the year of Skillzy – a freestyling, street-balling, panna boss man!

8 THE COMP WINNERS GET £10m!

If it wasn't good enough to just win the whole tournament, whoever comes out on top in July also gets a big, whopping pot filled with £10m. The epic prize will then be used to help fund the future of the game in that country. Nice one!

9 "LIVE IT. FOR REAL!"

That's the competition's official slogan, with the idea that this is an international tournament that can be enjoyed by hundreds of thousands of fans all around Europe with so many games being in different cities!

TURN OVER FOR MORE!

10 FRANCE ARE THE FAVOURITES!

The tournament is not until next summer but World Cup winners France have already been named as the team to beat. When you've got a front line of Kylian Mbappe and Antoine Griezmann what do you expect? Ballers for days!

11 TICKET TEKKERS!

You can expect some awesome atmospheres next summer. Why? Because 82% of tickets are being sold to proper fans of each country or the general public rather than posh business owners who don't care about the match. A record 19.3 million fans applied for tickets!

12 ENGLAND'S DREAM!

The Three Lions have played at nine European Championships in their history and never won it! The furthest they've gone is the semi-finals, but 2020 is different. They've never had a hungrier, more talented squad. It's finally coming home!

PAZ SAYS
This is England's best chance of winning a tournament since the golden generation of 2002-06 – can they go one stage further than the 2018 World Cup?

13 ITALY OPENER!

We know the tourney will be hosted by 12 different countries, but Rome, Italy, is the location for the first game of the competition. The epic Stadio Olimpico holds 72,000 people and is going to be pumping at the opening ceremony!

14 TALE OF THE TROPHY!

The Henri Delaunay Trophy, which is awarded to the winner of the European Championships, is named after, well, Henri Delaunay! Old Henners was the first General Secretary of UEFA and the bloke who came up with the idea for the tournament!

15 YOUNG EUROS!

If watching the men's tourney isn't enough for you, there are two wonderkid comps on, too! The U-19 Euros run from 19 July until 1 August in Northern Ireland, while the U-17 Euros in Estonia start on 1 May and end on 17 May. Happy football, readers!

16 NEW KITS GALORE!

Every international tournament brings out the best in kit makers – they rustle up some sick new summer styles that usually pop with colour so players can stand out. Euro 2020 will be no different – we're buzzing to see what drops!

17 CITY GUIDE!

Thinking of heading to a game abroad, but have no idea what to do there? Log on to uefa.com and they've very handily written city guides for every host nation, so you can sniff out the best pizza, merch shops and pick-up game spots!

18 FINAL FIGHT!

Traditionally, host nations automatically get a place at the competition finals, however in 2020, all 12 countries have been required to fight it out for a spot through standard qualification groups over the past year. Fair enough!

19 HOME COMFORTS!

There are some benefits to being a host nation, though! All 12 countries who have put forward a stadium for the tournament will get to play AT LEAST two games on home soil. Nice touch!

20 POWER RANKINGS!

On UEFA'S website, the stat boffins have been analysing every single player who has competed in international matches leading up to the tournament and ranked them using a clever points system. At the time of writing this, Jordan Pickford is the best player heading into Euro 2020, followed by Memphis Depay and Frenkie de Jong. Sick!

QUIZ ANSWERS

How well did you do? Check your scores below, quizzers!

A year in football!
From p16

1=B 2=C 3=B 4=C 5=B
6=B 7=B 8=B 9=B

MY SCORE [ANSWER] **OUT OF 9**

The Champions Quiz!
From p20

1=C 2=B 3=A 4=A 5=A
6=C 7=B 8=C 9=B

MY SCORE [ANSWER] **OUT OF 9**

Guess Who?
From p34

Player 1 Jonjo Shelvey
2 Andrew Robertson
3 Aymeric Laporte
4 Bernd Leno 5 Conor Coady
6 Lucas Digne

MY SCORE [ANSWER] **OUT OF 6**

MOTD Scrapbook Quiz
From p44

1 Aaron Creswell 2 Alex Scott
3 Olly Murs
4 Trent Alexander-Arnold
5 Lionel Messi

FANS The stars love Match of the Day mag!

the hunt for fast

6 Alex Greenwood
7 Harry Winks
8 Billy Wingrove
9 Alan Shearer 10 Kevin
De Bruyne 11 Adebayo
Akinfenwa 12 Sergio Aguero
13 Ruben Loftus-Cheek
14 Jez Lynch 15 Tekkerz Kid
16 Paulo Dybala 17 Dani Alves
18 Luke Shaw
19 Leah Williamson
20 Ben Shires

MY SCORE [ANSWER] **OUT OF 20**

The Weird & Wonderful Footy Quiz!
From p61

1=A 2=D 3=A
4=C 5=A 6=B
7=B 8=C 9=A
10=D 11=D 12=C
13=D 14=B 15=C
16=B 17=A 18=C
19=A 20 Dundee

MY SCORE [ANSWER] **OUT OF 20**

Quiz A Grown-Up!
From p72

1=C 2 Gabriel Batistuta
3 Thomas Brolin
4 Claudio Ranieri,
Carlo Ancelotti,
Roberto Mancini,
Antonio Conte
5 Everton & Sheffield
Wednesday
6 Stuart Pearce & Des Walker

MY SCORE [ANSWER] **OUT OF 6**

MATCH of the DAY

Write to us at...
Match of the Day magazine
Immediate Media, Vineyard House,
44 Brook Green, Hammersmith,
London, W6 7BT

Telephone 020 7150 5513
Email shout@motdmag.com
pazandketch@motdmag.com
Website motdmag.com

Match of the Day editor	Ian Foster
Annual editor	Mark Parry
Senior art editor	Blue Buxton
Annual designer	Steve Beech
Digital editor/senior writer	Matthew Ketchell
Features editor	Lee Stobbs
Group picture editor	Natasha Thompson
Picture editor	Jason Timson

Production editor	Neil Queen-Jones
Deputy production editor	Joe Shackley
Publishing consultant	Jaynie Bye
Editorial director	Corinna Shaffer
Annual images	Getty Images

BBC Books an imprint of Ebury Publishing 20 Vauxhall Bridge Road London SW1V 2SA. BBC Books is part of the Penguin Random House group of companies whose addresses can be found at global.penguinrandomhouse.com. Copyright © Match Of The Day magazine 2019. First published by BBC Books in 2019 www.penguin.co.uk. A CIP catalogue record for this book is available from the British Library. ISBN 9781785944550. Commissioning editor: Albert DePetrillo; project editor: Daniel Sorensen; production: Phil Spencer. Printed and bound in Italy by Elcograf S.p.A. Penguin Random House is committed to a sustainable future for our business our readers and our planet. This book is made from Forest Stewardship Council® certified paper.

BBC

The licence to publish this magazine was acquired from BBC Studios by Immediate Media Company on 1 November 2011. We remain committed to making a magazine of the highest editorial quality one that complies with BBC editorial and commercial guidelines and connects with BBC programmes.

Match Of The Day Magazine is is published by Immediate Media Company London Limited under licence from BBC Studios. © Immediate Media Company London Limited 2019.

DON'T EXPECT ME TO PUT THE BINS OUT ON A TUESDAY!

I'M TOO BUSY READING...

MATCH of the DAY
magazine

GET YOUR MOTD MAG FIX EVERY WEEK!*

*bin bags not included

MY PREDICTIONS FOR 2019-20!

YOUR FACT FILE!

NAME:	AGE:
HOMETOWN:	
FAVOURITE TEAM:	
FAVOURITE PLAYER:	

STICK A PHOTO OF YOURSELF HERE!

Q1 WHO WILL WIN THE PREMIER LEAGUE?

The final Premier League match of the season is on Sunday 17 May – so who will be celebrating?

1 ....
2 ....

2018-19: MAN. CITY

Premier League

PAZ SAYS
Last season's title race was a madness – let's hope for more of the same!

Q2 WHO WILL BE PFA PLAYER OF THE YEAR?

This is the award voted for by all Prem players – will it be a Liverpool player for the THIRD year in a row?

....

2018-19: VIRGIL VAN DIJK

Q3 WHO WILL WIN THE PREM GOLDEN BOOT?

Three players shared it last season for the first time in 20 years – they scored 22 goals each!

....

2018-19: P. AUBAMEYANG, SADIO MANE, MO SALAH

Q4 WHO WILL WIN THE EFL CUP?

Man. City have won four of the last six EFL Cup finals. Will they do it again on 1 March 2020?

....

2018-19: MAN. CITY